EASY AS ABC

Qq

Warren Rylands and Samantha Nugent

LET'S READ
AV²
BY WEIGL™
ADDED VALUE • AUDIO VISUAL

AV² provides enriched content that supplements and complements this book. Weigl's AV² books strive to create inspired learning and engage young minds in a total learning experience.

Your AV² Media Enhanced books come alive with...

 Audio
Listen to sections of the book read aloud.

 Video
Watch informative video clips.

 Embedded Weblinks
Gain additional information for research.

 Try This!
Complete activities and hands-on experiments.

 Key Words
Study vocabulary, and complete a matching word activity.

 Quizzes
Test your knowledge.

 Slide Show
View images and captions, and prepare a presentation.

... and much, much more!

Go to **www.av2books.com**, and enter this book's unique code.

BOOK CODE

B863635

AV² by Weigl brings you media enhanced books that support active learning.

Published by AV² by Weigl
350 5th Avenue, 59th Floor
New York, NY 10118

Website: www.av2books.com

Library of Congress Control Number: 2015940620

ISBN 978-1-4896-3533-4 (hardcover)
ISBN 978-1-4896-3535-8 (single user eBook)
ISBN 978-1-4896-3536-5 (multi-user eBook)

Printed in the United States of America in Brainerd, Minnesota
1 2 3 4 5 6 7 8 9 0 19 18 17 16 15

052015
WEP050815

Project Coordinator: Katie Gillespie   Art Director: Terry Paulhus

Weigl acknowledges Getty Images and iStock as the primary image suppliers for this title.

CONTENTS

Let's explore the letter

The uppercase letter Q looks like this

The lowercase letter q looks like this

The letter **q** can start many words.

quilt

quiz

question

queen

quiet

7

The letter q can be inside a word.

aqua

squash

squid

toque

The letter q can be at the end of a word.

umiaq

suq

Iraq

Many names start with an uppercase Q.

Queenie

Quigley likes to surf.

Quinn can fly.

Quincy has a long tail.

Quentin loves to read.

13

The letter q makes one sound.

queen

quail

The word queen
has the q sound.

The word quail
has the q sound.

Many words have

the **q** sound.

square

quick

squirrel

liquid

quake

The letter q almost always comes before the letter u.

equal

quack

squiggle

quart

quarter

19

Having Fun with Q

Quinn is the queen of
the squids.

Queen Quinn was going on a
quest to find quiet squash. She
had to be as quick as a quail.

Quincy had to take a quiz
before he could join the quest.

The **q**uestions were difficult for **Q**uincy.

Quincy **q**uacked with joy when he passed the **q**uiz.

The alphabet has 26 letters.

Q is the seventeenth letter in the alphabet.

Aa Bb Cc Dd Ee

Ff Gg Hh Ii Jj Kk

Ll Mm Nn Oo Pp

Qq Rr Ss Tt Uu Vv

Ww Xx Yy Zz

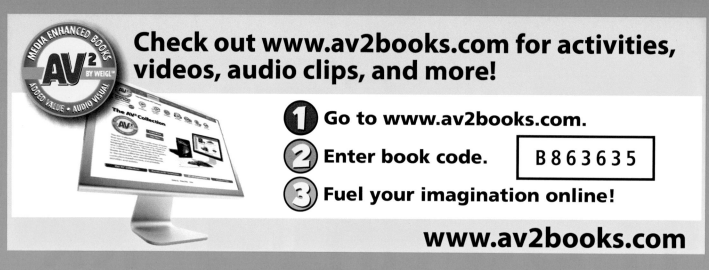
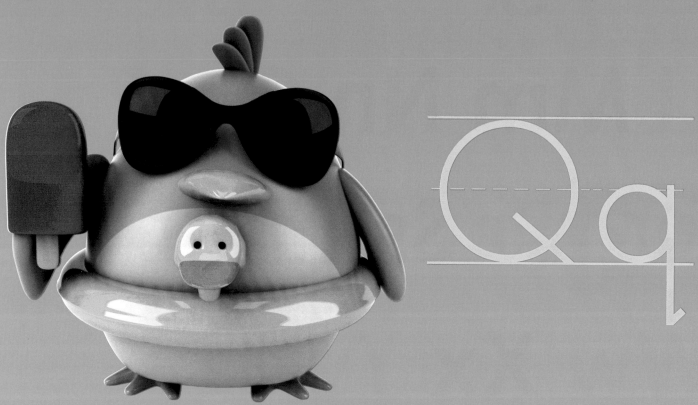

Qq